Sleep Meditation for Anxiety Relief

Start Sleeping Smarter and Declutter by Following Hypnosis & Meditation Scripts for a Night's Rest

Harmony Academy

Table of Contents

Table of Contents
Introduction
Chapter 1: Sleep Hypnosis Script
Chapter 2: Anxiety Hypnosis Script
Chapter 3: Sleep Meditation Script
Chapter 4: Anxiety Meditation Script

Hey, it's Harmony Academy,

Before we start, I want to tell you about an exclusive offer just for readers of this book...

When you start meditating, the one thing that you must know is how to meditate correctly. If you don't then you are making something that should be easy super tough.

It surprises a lot of people when they actually talk to an expert and discuss how to meditate properly, and they're told they're doing it all wrong. Then when they follow certain teachings they see the wonders of how meditating properly the effects it actually has on them.

You may ask so how do I start meditating properly, right?

For most people they would be stopped there at that very question, but luckily for you, I have partnered up with Absolute Meditation. Who are giving away their highly rated course that will give you all of the step-by-step teachings for teaching you how to meditate correctly!

Best thing about this exclusive offer is it 100% FREE, no-strings-attached. Absolute Meditation usually charges $297 for this exact same course to their customers

All you need to do to claim your FREE Meditation course; is type in on your search browsers URL – free.absolutemeditation.com

Once you are on the web page, fill out the required information that Absolute Meditations asks for; this should only take less than 1 minute of your time. Then straight away in your email inbox you will receive the life changing course that has helped 10,000's of people around the world.

Before reading any further, please do this NOW as we may refer back to some of the units in the course throughout this book!

free.absolutemeditation.com

Introduction

Technology is a wonderful thing. It's the reason these words are reaching you now. Advancements have made things possible that societies of the past could never have imagined. We live longer, get information at the touch of a button, and can stay in touch with loved ones across the world easily.

Life has become much more convenient at a faster pace, but moving at such a fast pace has its downfalls. Our brains are constantly going, thoughts running through our minds faster and faster. We also have more worries than ever before. Life moves at a much faster pace than it ever has, and we have to keep up or face the consequences of falling behind. Catching up can seem impossible.

Even if worries don't keep you awake at night, your brain may continue to work too quickly for you to fall asleep. Have you ever felt so tired, staring at the little red numbers on your alarm clock, watching the numbers slowly march forward? You might get frustrated as you continue to lay awake, your impending wakeup alarm looming closer as your brain refuses to be quiet.

This is a very common problem, but you have the power to fix it. Meditation and hypnosis are a wonderful way to teach your brain how to slow down. This book contains some hypnosis and guided meditations to help you learn how to use mindfulness to get some well deserved rest.

Chapter 1: Sleep Hypnosis Script

The purpose of this hypnosis session is to help you get to sleep easier. The best time to use this is right before you go to bed.

Lay down and get comfortable. If you sleep on your side, it's fine to lay down in that position. If you want to sleep with a blanket on, go ahead and get under the covers now.

Once you're comfortable, close your eyes.

Do a scan of your body. If you feel any tension, release it. Are your neck and shoulders tense? Let them relax. You might be clenching your jaw, so release that tension.

Once you feel relaxed, shift your focus to your breath.

Breathe in through your nose. One. Two. Three. Four.

Hold. One. Two. Three.

Breathe out through your mouth. One. Two. Three. Four. Five. Six.

Good. Stay with me and continue breathing.

In. One. Two. Three. Four.

Hold. One. Two. Three.

Out. One. Two. Three. Four. Five. Six.

In. One. Two. Three. Four.
Hold. One. Two. Three.
Out. One. Two. Three. Four. Five. Six.
In. One. Two. Three. Four.
Hold. One. Two. Three.
Out. One. Two. Three. Four. Five. Six.
In. One. Two. Three. Four.
Hold. One. Two. Three.
Out. One. Two. Three. Four. Five. Six.
In. One. Two. Three. Four.
Hold. One. Two. Three.
Out. One. Two. Three. Four. Five. Six.
In. One. Two. Three. Four.
Hold. One. Two. Three.
Out. One. Two. Three. Four. Five. Six.
In. One. Two. Three. Four.
Hold. One. Two. Three.
Out. One. Two. Three. Four. Five. Six.
In. One. Two. Three. Four.
Hold. One. Two. Three.
Out. One. Two. Three. Four. Five. Six.

Now envision yourself floating in the middle of a lake on a calm night. In your mind's eye, look up at the sky. Stars stretch as far as you can see, and there's no light or noise of the city. It's just you and the calm rhythm of nature.

Listen. What do you hear? Frogs croak on the lake shore, and waves lap gently at the sand. An owl leaves its question echoing in the air.

As I begin to count in a moment, imagine yourself sinking into the water, deeper and deeper.

Ten. You begin to sink. You are under water, but can breathe and are perfectly safe. You feel no worry.

Nine. You sink a bit deeper, the quietness of the water a relaxing lullaby.

Eight. Sinking deeper, feeling more relaxed.

Seven. You begin to feel yourself drifting at the edge of consciousness, in that pleasant place between dreams and real life.

Six. Go a bit deeper.

Five. The water is warm and comforting.

Four. You are nearing the bottom of the lake now, just sink a bit deeper.

Three. So close.

Two. You feel soft sand touching your back, cradling you more comfortably than any mattress.

One. You are completely relaxed and finally drift off to sleep.

It's okay if you aren't quite asleep yet. If you need to sink deeper into relaxation, return to your breathing.

In. One. Two. Three. Four.
Hold. One. Two. Three.
Out. One. Two. Three. Four. Five. Six.
You continue to sink deeper, deeper, and deeper.
In. One. Two. Three. Four.
Hold. One. Two. Three.
Out. One. Two. Three. Four. Five. Six.
Keep breathing until you finally drift off into your land of dreams.
In. One. Two. Three. Four.
Hold. One. Two. Three.
Out. One. Two. Three. Four. Five. Six.
In. One. Two. Three. Four.
Hold. One. Two. Three.
Out. One. Two. Three. Four. Five. Six.
In. One. Two. Three. Four.
Hold. One. Two. Three.
Out. One. Two. Three. Four. Five. Six.

Come back to this session anytime you need help sleeping and it will become easier each time to drift deep, deep, deeper.

Chapter 2: Anxiety Hypnosis Script

This is a short hypnosis session to help you reduce anxiety. You can listen to this session whenever you want, just find somewhere to relax and take some time for yourself where you won't be interrupted. You can choose to follow this session pretty much anywhere you feel comfortable, but please never listen to meditation or hypnosis tapes while driving or operating heavy machinery.

To begin, sit with your back straight. If you're sitting in a chair, plant your feet firmly on the ground. If you are sitting on the floor, cross your legs. Choose a position that's most comfortable for you.

Close your eyes.

Take a deep breath in through your nose. Breathe deeper until you can't breathe anymore in.

Now exhale from your mouth in a quick rush.

Breathe in through your nose again, slower this time. One. Two. Three. Four.

Breathe out through your mouth. One. Two. Three. Four. Five. Six.

In. One. Two. Three. Four.

Out. One. Two. Three. Four. Five. Six.

In. One. Two. Three. Four.

Out. One. Two. Three. Four. Five. Six.

As you continue to breathe, imagine yourself sinking into the earth. It's a warm and comforting sensation. I will count backwards from ten, and when I reach one, you will be in a very deep state of relaxation.

Ten. Sinking deeper. A peaceful darkness envelops you, inviting you to relax.

Nine.

Eight.

Seven.

Six.

Five. Your body is relaxed and free of tension.

Four.

Three.

Two.

One. You sink deeper still, and find yourself in a state of profound relaxation.

At this moment, you have no responsibilities or worries. Only this moment and your consciousness exist.

Repeat after me, out loud or in your head.

I am free. There is nothing to worry about right now. I'm allowed to spend time on myself.

Good. Now envision a box in front of you. What does your box look like? Perhaps it's a simple cardboard box, without any embellishments. Maybe it's a wooden box with a metal clasp. Whatever your box looks like, I want you to picture it in your mind.

Pick up the box, feel it in your hands. It is sturdy, and you know that anything you store in this box will be safe until you return to it.

Set the box back down and open it. Picture the inside of the box. Do you have the image in your mind's eye? Good, you're doing great.

Now shift your thoughts to anything that may be causing anxiety. Do you have a test coming up? Maybe your neighbors have been causing trouble, or you have a stressful deadline coming up soon. Whatever your worry is, imagine it leaving your brain and becoming a glowing orb in front of you.

Hold it in your hands. It's so small and isn't all that scary now. Place the orb in the box and take a deep breath. The orb will stay inside the box, safe and sound until you're ready to revisit it.

Take a few moments and do the same thing with any other worries.

Close the lid of your box. I want you to think of a word to associate with this box. It can be anything, but it should be easy to remember. In your mind's eye, take a marker and write your word on top of the box. Your box cannot be opened without this word.

When you feel ready to look in the box or when you want to put more in the box, say your word and you can change the contents.

We're nearing the end of this hypnosis session now, and I will count up from ten to bring you out of your trance.

One. Feel yourself rising from the deep place of relaxation you've been in.

Two.

Three.

Four.

Five. We're halfway to the surface.

Six.

Seven.

Eight.

Nine.

Ten. You are fully aware of your surroundings and you feel alert and ready to continue your day. Open your eyes.

Any time that you feel anxious and need to put those feelings in a safe place, you will have your word. Your word will allow you to rummage through the contents of your box, add to it, and look at those worries in a safe place when you're ready.

If you feel you need to strengthen your connection to the box, you can do this hypnosis session again any time.

Hey, it's Harmony Academy,

As mentioned at the start of this book, you have an exclusive offer available to you for a short period of time.

In case you forgot to claim your 100% FREE, no strings attached Meditation course by Absolute Meditation.

Please can you make sure to do so NOW!

It will be pivotal to have this course available at all times as when meditating, the Meditation course for beginners will guide you to implement these strategies in a quick and effective manner.

In case you forgot how to claim your FREE copy of meditation for beginner's course, is type in on your search browser URL – free.absolutemeditation.com

Remember, before reading any further, please do this NOW as we may refer back to parts of the course throughout this book!

free.absolutemeditation.com

Chapter 3: Sleep Meditation Script

This guided meditation is meant to help you fall asleep more easily. It's best to listen to this meditation when you've gotten into bed for the night or if you wake up and can't fall asleep again.

Lay down on your bed and find a comfortable position. Laying on your back is best, but it's perfectly fine if another position is more comfortable for you.

Begin by doing some deep breathing. Breathe in through your nose. One. Two. Three.

Breathe out through your mouth. One. Two. Three. Four. Five. Six.

In. One. Two. Three.

Out. One. Two. Three. Four. Five. Six.

In. One. Two. Three.

Out. One. Two. Three. Four. Five. Six.

In. One. Two. Three.

Out. One. Two. Three. Four. Five. Six.

In. One. Two. Three.

Out. One. Two. Three. Four. Five. Six.
In. One. Two. Three.
Out. One. Two. Three. Four. Five. Six.

You should be feeling very relaxed now. We're going to relax every part of your body now, one by one.

Start at your feet. Feel your toes, wiggle them a little bit. Find a comfortable position for them. Imagine that your feet are growing very heavy now. It should feel as if your feet are being filled with concrete or sand.

Let the weight move slowly up your legs. First your ankles. Then you begin to feel it seeping into your shins, then your knees. Your thighs begin to fill with heaviness next.

Let the heaviness shift up into your hips and pelvis.

The comfortable weight is at your lower stomach now, moving up across your belly button and up into your chest. You are in control of how quickly or slowly it's moving.

As it moves into your shoulders and neck, give it some extra time to really fill that area and release any tension. Once your shoulders feel very relaxed, allow the heaviness to start moving down into your arms.

Feel it work its way past your elbow, into your wrists, and finally to the tips of your fingers.

Next, allow the weight to move up into your head, and fill your body completely.

Stay with the heaviness for a moment, focusing on your breathing.

In. One. Two. Three.
Out. One. Two. Three. Four. Five. Six.
In. One. Two. Three.
Out. One. Two. Three. Four. Five. Six.
In. One. Two. Three.
Out. One. Two. Three. Four. Five. Six.
In. One. Two. Three.
Out. One. Two. Three. Four. Five. Six.
In. One. Two. Three.
Out. One. Two. Three. Four. Five. Six.
In. One. Two. Three.
Out. One. Two. Three. Four. Five. Six.
In. One. Two. Three.
Out. One. Two. Three. Four. Five. Six.
In. One. Two. Three.
Out. One. Two. Three. Four. Five. Six.
In. One. Two. Three.

Out. One. Two. Three. Four. Five. Six.

Now allow the heaviness to begin flowing out of your body slowly. As it leaves, your muscles are left feeling completely relaxed and light.

Now return to your breathing, and let your mind quiet.

In. One. Two. Three.

Out. One. Two. Three. Four. Five. Six.

It's okay if a thought drifts across your mind. Acknowledge it, tell yourself it's okay, and let it pass.

In. One. Two. Three.

Out. One. Two. Three. Four. Five. Six.

In. One. Two. Three.

Out. One. Two. Three. Four. Five. Six.

In. One. Two. Three.

Out. One. Two. Three. Four. Five. Six.

You're doing great. If you find your mind wandering, return your attention to your breath. Feel the sensation as you inhale. The rise of your chest that comes with it. Feel the air moving through your throat as you exhale. Your breath is your friend.

You should feel very relaxed and your mind should be quiet now. You will be able to slip into a deep, relaxing slumber easily, and when you wake up you will feel refreshed.

Come back to this exercise any time you need help reaching a deep state of calm. Every time you do this, you will get better at it, and rest will come easier and quicker every time.

Chapter 4: Anxiety Meditation Script

This guided meditation is meant to help you let go of your anxiety. If meditation is new to you, don't worry about being perfect. Meditation takes practice to get better. Even if you have to redirect your thoughts every few seconds, you are still improving.

For this session, you should find a quiet place to sit or lay down. Turn off your phone and make sure you won't be disturbed.

If you choose to sit, rest your hands on your knees and keep your back straight.

If you would rather lay down, find a comfortable position that you can stay in. It's best if you don't move much during this session, but don't worry if you have an itch or need to shift your body. Moving a bit is perfectly fine.

Find a fixed point and let your gaze soften as you keep looking at it. Blink a few times slowly. When you're ready, close your eyes.

Notice how your body is feeling. Are you holding tension in any of your muscles? Pay attention to your shoulders, and release any tension you find there. Shift your focus to your jaw. Are you clenching your teeth? Relax and let the tension ease away.

Take a deep breath through your nose. One. Two. Three.

Hold the breath. One. Two.

Breathe out through your mouth. One. Two. Three. Four.

In through the nose. One. Two. Three.

Hold. One. Two.

Out through the mouth. One. Two. Three. Four.

In. One. Two. Three.

Hold. One. Two.

Out. One. Two. Three. Four.

Now I want you to imagine you're walking through a forest, bare footed.

Feel the dirt of the path beneath your feet. Wiggle your toes, feeling Mother Nature reaching out to connect with you.

Gently raise your gaze to the leaves above you. What do you see? Maybe you see a canopy of beautiful green, with muted rays of light filtering through. Watch the particles of dust catching the light as they float without a care in the world.

Listen to the sounds of the forest around you. Birds sing in the distance. Crickets chirp in the lush foliage just off the path.

Breathe in nature all around you. The forest moves with its own rhythm, everything in perfect balance.

Right now you can forget everything outside of this forest. You are part of the universe, and you are part of that beautiful balance.

Take a step further down the path. Ahead you see a glint of light, and a stream comes into focus. As you draw closer, you can hear the melody of the current. The sound of rushing water soothes you.

Sit down beside the stream. Dip your toes in the water and wiggle them. How does it feel? Can you feel the cool water lapping around your foot?

A gentle wind rises and leaves begin to fall and float in the stream.

Take a deep breath.

Inhale. One. Two. Three.

Hold. One. Two.

Exhale. One. Two. Three. Four.

We're going to keep going for five breaths. Stay with me as I count.

In. One. Two. Three.
Hold. One. Two.
Out. One. Two. Three. Four.
In. One. Two. Three.
Hold. One. Two.
Out. One. Two. Three. Four.
In. One. Two. Three.
Hold. One. Two.
Out. One. Two. Three. Four.
In. One. Two. Three.
Hold. One. Two.
Out. One. Two. Three. Four.
In. One. Two. Three.
Hold. One. Two.
Out. One. Two. Three. Four.

Good. Keep breathing and empty your mind. Let go of any of your worries. You don't need to think of anything right now. This is your time.

If you find your mind wandering, return your attention to your breath. Don't be discouraged by stray thoughts. Let them float across your mind. Acknowledge them and let them go. You can come back to these thoughts later at a time that's better for you.

When you're ready, shift your awareness back to your physical body. Wiggle your fingers, feeling the sensation coming back into focus.

Wiggle your toes and stretch your spine.

When you're solidly back in the room and feel ready to, open your eyes.

You should feel relaxed and rested. You can come back to this session anytime you need to. Each time you practice your meditation, it'll become easier and quicker to slip into a state of relaxation.

If you enjoyed this book in anyway, an honest review is always appreciated!

Hey, it's Harmony Academy,

Firstly thanks for completing our book.

Remember, there are particular tools that you need not just to make meditation easier, but make it more effective.

The first crucial tool you will need to make sure you have, so you know how to meditate properly, is Meditation for Beginners by Absolute Meditation.

As when meditating, the one thing that you must know how to do first to claim all the benefits of meditation is how to actually meditate properly.

You may ask so how do I start meditating properly, right?

For most people they would be stopped there at that very question, but luckily for you, I have partnered up with Absolute Meditation. Who are giving away their highly rated course that will give you all of the step-by-step teachings for teaching you how to meditate correctly!

Best thing about this exclusive offer is it 100% FREE, no-strings-attached. Absolute Meditation usually charges $297 for this exact same course to their customers

All you need to do to claim your FREE Meditation course; is type in on your search browsers URL – free.absolutemeditation.com

Good luck on your journey and enjoy the course!

free.absolutemeditation.com

CPSIA information can be obtained
at www.ICGtesting.com
Printed in the USA
LVHW081141031120
670573LV00004B/662